Scary Creatures
RATS

Written by
Dr. Gerald Legg

Illustrated by
Mark Bergin
and Bob Hersey

W
FRANKLIN WATTS
A Division of Scholastic Inc.
NEW YORK • TORONTO • LONDON • AUCKLAND • SYDNEY
MEXICO CITY • NEW DELHI • HONG KONG
DANBURY, CONNECTICUT

Created and designed by
David Salariya

Author:

Dr. Gerald Legg holds a doctorate in zoology from Manchester University. He worked in West Africa for several years as a lecturer and rainforest researcher. His current position is biologist at the Booth Museum of Natural History in Brighton, England.

Artists:

Mark Bergin was born in Hastings, England, in 1961. He studied at Eastbourne College of Art and has illustrated many children's nonfiction books. He lives in Bexhill-on-Sea with his wife and three children.

Bob Hersey has worked in many mediums, including designing 3-dimensional models, artwork for advertising, and illustrating children's books. He lives in Sevenoaks, Kent.

Additional Artists:

Robert Morton

Carolyn Scrace

David Stewart

Series Creator:

David Salariya was born in Dundee, Scotland. In 1989 he established The Salariya Book Company. He has illustrated a wide range of books and has created many new series for publishers in the U.K. and overseas. He lives in Brighton with his wife, illustrator Shirley Willis, and their son.

Editor: Karen Barker Smith

Picture Research: Nicky Roe

Created, designed, and produced by
The Salariya Book Company Ltd
Book House
25 Marlborough Place
Brighton BN1 1UB

Visit the Salariya Book Company at
www.salariya.com

A CIP catalog record for this title is available from the Library of Congress.

ISBN 0-531-14671-5 (Lib. Bdg.)
ISBN 0-531-14852-1 (Pbk.)

Published in the United States by Franklin Watts
A Division of Scholastic Inc.
90 Sherman Turnpike
Danbury, CT 06816

Printed in China.

Printed on paper from sustainable forests.

Photo Credits:

Stephen Dalton, NHPA: 8, 9, 10, 11, 12, 13, 22
Nick Garbutt, NHPA: 24
Pavel German, NHPA: 27
Angela Hampton, RSPCA Photolibrary: 20
Daniel Heuclin, NHPA: 21
Haroldo Palo Jr., NHPA: 25
Andy Roe: 16

Contents

What Are Rats?

Rats are a type of **mammal** called a rodent. Most rodents are small creatures. They range from the 0.2 ounce (6 g) harvest mouse to the 176 pound (80 kg) capybara. The capybara lives in South America and is the largest rodent alive. To avoid being hunted by other animals, most rodents are **nocturnal**.

Are these animals rodents?

Mole
Moles are small, have a short tail, and like to burrow.

Arctic lemming
Lemmings have dense fur to keep them warm as they burrow through snow.

Chipmunk
Chipmunks are ground squirrels that live and store their food in underground burrows.

Yes, all of these animals are rodents.

Over 40% of all mammals are rodents. Squirrels are rodents that live in trees. They have long tails that help them balance as they climb.

Red squirrel

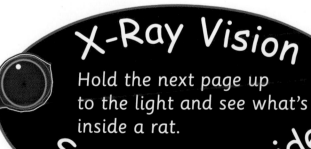

X-Ray Vision
Hold the next page up to the light and see what's inside a rat.

See what's inside

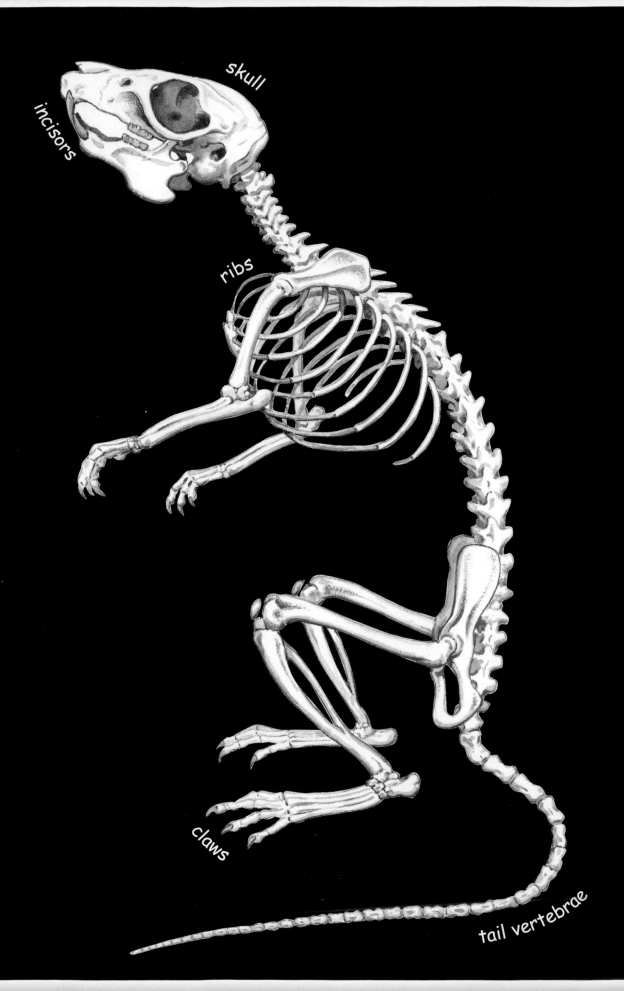

What's Inside a Rat?

Rats have long tails that help them balance when walking along narrow ledges or jumping from place to place. They have excellent sight, and a good sense of smell and hearing.

Rats' jaw muscles are strong. Their front teeth, the incisors, are ideal for gnawing and digging. The molars at the back of the mouth grind up food. Their short legs and feet, with five toes and claws, make rats good at running, turning, climbing, and swimming.

Rats can eat food that other mammals cannot. They have self-sharpening, curved incisors that are hard enough to eat the toughest meal.

Cutaway of a rat, showing its insides

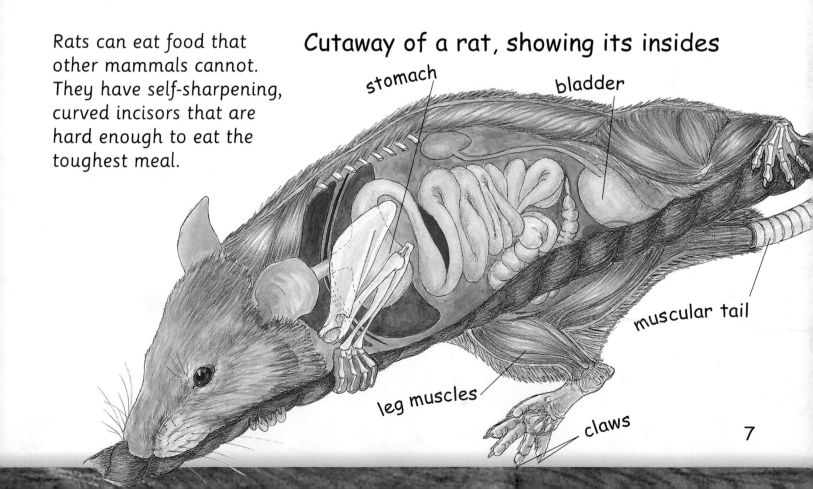

stomach

bladder

muscular tail

leg muscles

claws

What Do Baby Rats Look Like?

Female rats can have up to seven litters each year, giving birth to four to 12 babies each time. Baby rats are born blind, naked, and helpless. They are dependent on their mother for the first few weeks of life. At two weeks old, their eyes open. By five weeks they are **weaned** and young females can start breeding.

Did You Know?

In a **colony** of naked mole rats, only one female breeds. She is called the "queen" and the other rats are called "workers."

8 Brown rat and her young in their nest

Did You Know?

If her nest is disturbed, a mother rat will carefully carry her babies, one by one, to a safer place.

Brown rat carrying young in her mouth 9

Why Are Rats Scary?

Rats are active at night and in dark places such as sewers. Many rats carry **parasites** and diseases. Gnawing with their powerful teeth causes a lot of damage. Rats will fight for their lives if they are in danger and may attack pets and people. It is not surprising, then, that many people fear and hate rats.

Did You Know?

A rat's chewing through electrical cables can start dangerous fires, but they may also get electrocuted. Rats have even chewed through dams!

Pair of brown rats sniffing out garbage

Brown rat leaping from a garbage bin

Some studies claim that there are five rats for every human being on Earth. There are so many rats that it is thought wherever you are standing on land, there will be a rat within 49 feet (15 m).

Did You Know?

If a rat does not have enough hard things to gnaw on, its teeth can become overgrown. If they are not worn down the teeth can grow so much that the rat cannot eat at all. The teeth may even keep growing into the roof of the mouth.

Are Rats Dirty?

Very few **species** of rats are dangerous, harmful, or dirty. Rats often live and feed in dirty places, but they keep their fur and whiskers clean by **grooming**. Towns and cities are good places for rats to find food and shelter. However, they pick up all kinds of diseases on their feet and bodies that no amount of grooming can remove.

Did You Know?

A rat is able to climb and swim through toilet waste pipes to emerge in a bathroom. It will then set off in search of food.

12 Brown rats raiding sacks of grain

Brown rat in a pantry

When they enter homes, restaurants, and other buildings, rats can **contaminate** food and the surroundings with disease from their urine and feces.

There are hundreds of water pipes and tunnels under buildings and roads that carry sewage and contain electrical cables. These make perfect homes for rats and allow them to travel around easily. As they explore and find food in people's garbage they pick up diseases and parasites.

Do rats carry diseases?

Sewage workers, sugarcane workers, and people doing watersports (above) on lakes and rivers can catch Weil's disease. Rats pass on this disease in their urine.

Yes, rats carry diseases.

Are Rats Killers?

Diseases carried by rats have caused millions of deaths around the world. The bubonic **plague epidemic** of 1347, known as the Black Death, killed 75 million people worldwide. In 1665 there was a second epidemic, the Great Plague. A third outbreak of plague began in 1850 in China and slowly spread to India, Hong Kong, Hawaii, and San Francisco. By 1899, about 120 million people had died from the disease.

The plague is actually carried by the rat flea. The fleas live on rats and then come into contact with people. When a flea bites a person, the disease is passed to them.

rat flea

black rat

Black Death victims were collected in carts

Did You Know?

The plague disease is very old. The 5,200-year-old mummy of Pharaoh Rameses V showed that he had died of the disease. The disease is still around today.

Plague pit for Black Death victims

A 17th-century nursery rhyme, that is still sung today, is thought to be based on the plague outbreaks: "Ring around the rosie" describes the early sign of the disease, a red skin rash. "A pocket full o' posies" refers to the flowers that people believed would protect them from the plague. "Ashes, ashes, we all fall down" – ashes refers to the cremated bodies of the plague victims, and falling down represents dying.

So many people died during the Black Death that victims had to be buried in pits (above) instead of proper graves.

Where Do Rats Live?

The two main species of rat that live alongside people are brown and black rats. Brown, or Norway, rats are common around farms and in cities. City rats enjoy luxury living with plenty of places to live and lots of food. They breed very quickly. In 1997, an estimated 28 million rats were living in New York City.

X-Ray Vision

Hold the next page up to the light and see where rats can be found.

See what's inside

A barn – a typical **habitat** for rats in the countryside

Do Rats Have Enemies?

In the wild, rats are preyed upon by cats, dogs, foxes, birds, and other carnivores. However, people are rats' main enemy. In the past, small dogs called terriers were bred especially for catching rats. Traps and poisons are also used to control them.

Modern rat catchers are called pest controllers or exterminators (right). They use poison baits, gas, and traps to catch and kill rats.

Do Rats Make Good Pets?

Victorian rat catchers used to keep the unusually colored rats that they found. They then bred and sold them. Today there are brown, white, **pied**, brown and white, **albino**, and many more types of pet rats. These intelligent and friendly creatures enjoy human company and are easily trained.

Did You Know?

In the early 20th century, the author Beatrix Potter kept rats. She wrote about them in her children's stories.

A rat kept as a pet (below) needs a lot of space and attention and will usually live to be two or three years old.

Rats like people and are clever and easy to breed. They have become a favorite with scientists. Scientists use specially bred, clean rats (left) to help make medicines and to study behavioral and medical problems. Over 20 million rats are bred in U.S. laboratories every year.

Rats in a laboratory cage

 Did You Know?

In 1961, before humans had traveled into space, the French sent a rat called Hector into space in a capsule. He returned safely to Earth.

Rat being prepared for space

How Do Rats Travel Long Distances?

Rats are very intelligent and **adapt** to their **environment** well. From the earliest days of human exploration, rats have stowed away on ships and traveled the world. As people discovered new lands and places to live, so did rats. In some places, where there were never rats before, they have taken over.

Did You Know?

Rats were probably brought over to the United States accidentally in 1775.

Black rat on a ship's rope

Rats originally traveled onboard sailing ships (above). Today, they are accidentally carried by cargo ships and liners all over the world.

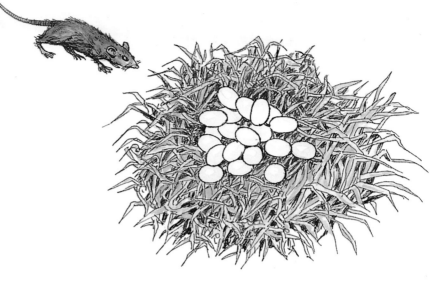

Rats can have a terrible effect on places where there were no rats before. Local animals often do not have any defense against the rats. The eggs and chicks of ground-nesting birds are easy **prey**. Many species have become **extinct** this way.

Did You Know?

Hawsers (thick ropes that tie ships to the harborside) are used by rats to get on and off ships. Because of this, the ropes that sailors use to climb the rigging are called ratlines.

Poisons have been developed to deal with the growing number of rats. One poison, called Warfarin, was invented in 1950 and has been very effective. Now "super-rats" have evolved that do not appear to be harmed by it.

Are There Different Types of Rats?

Over 135 types of rodents are called rats, but this does not mean that they are closely related to each other. Most rodents have been named "rat" because they look like rats. Some species are very common and others are near extinction.

Kangaroo rat

Kangaroo rats (above) are excellent jumpers, and have powerful back legs, long tails for balancing, and short front legs for landing. They like dry, grassy, and desert areas and are found throughout North America.

The giant jumping rat, or votsotsa, is more like a rabbit than a rat. It is **endangered**.

Endangered Madagascan giant jumping rat

Rice rat

Rats live in all kinds of **habitats**, from wet and marshy regions to deserts. Rats are nocturnal, sleeping in the shade or down a burrow during the heat of the day. They come out at night to feed. Many are good at climbing trees, while others like to live on the ground. Some, such as sand rats, can escape from **predators** by jumping.

Rice rats (above) like marshy, swampy areas where they can dive and swim.

 Did You Know?

Stick-nest rats in Australia build huge nests from piles of sticks, sometimes up to 5 feet (1.5 m) tall.

More Rats

The largest group of rats includes the two most widely known species, the black, or roof, rat and brown, or Norway, rat. Scientists call them *Rattus* and over 570 different forms of *Rattus* have been discovered. Brown and black rats like living near people in the countryside, towns, and cities.

Did You Know?

The mole rats that are found in Europe, the Middle East, and western Asia live in underground burrows and are blind.

Black rats (right) first came from Asia and the Far East.

Black rat

Brown, or Norway, rats (left) originally lived only in eastern Asia and Japan. They are now found virtually everywhere in the world except the Antarctic.

Brown rat

African bush rats (left) are excellent climbers and have very long tails to help them balance.

African bush rat

Bamboo rats (right) live in Asia. They feed at night on bamboo and are sometimes eaten by giant pandas.

Bamboo rat

African mole rats (left) are like American pocket gophers. They use their powerful feet and large incisors to dig burrows.

African mole rat

27

Rats Around the World

Different kinds of rats can be found throughout most of the world, in the Arctic, Africa, the Americas, Europe, Asia, India, and Australia.

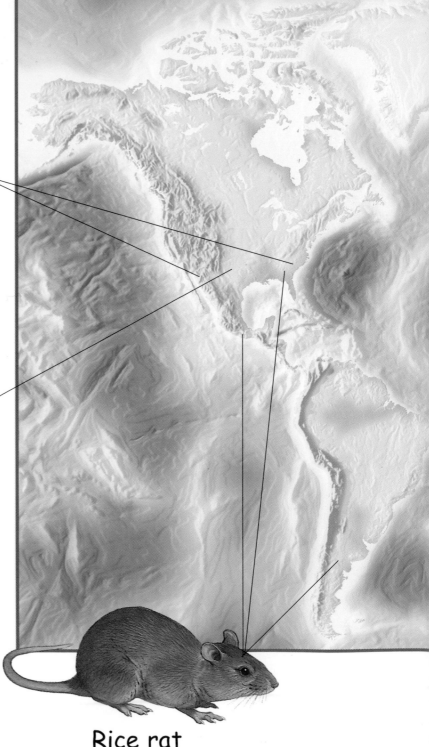

Black rat

Kangaroo rat

Rice rats (right) are found in the southern U.S., Central America, South America, and the Galapagos Islands.

Rice rat

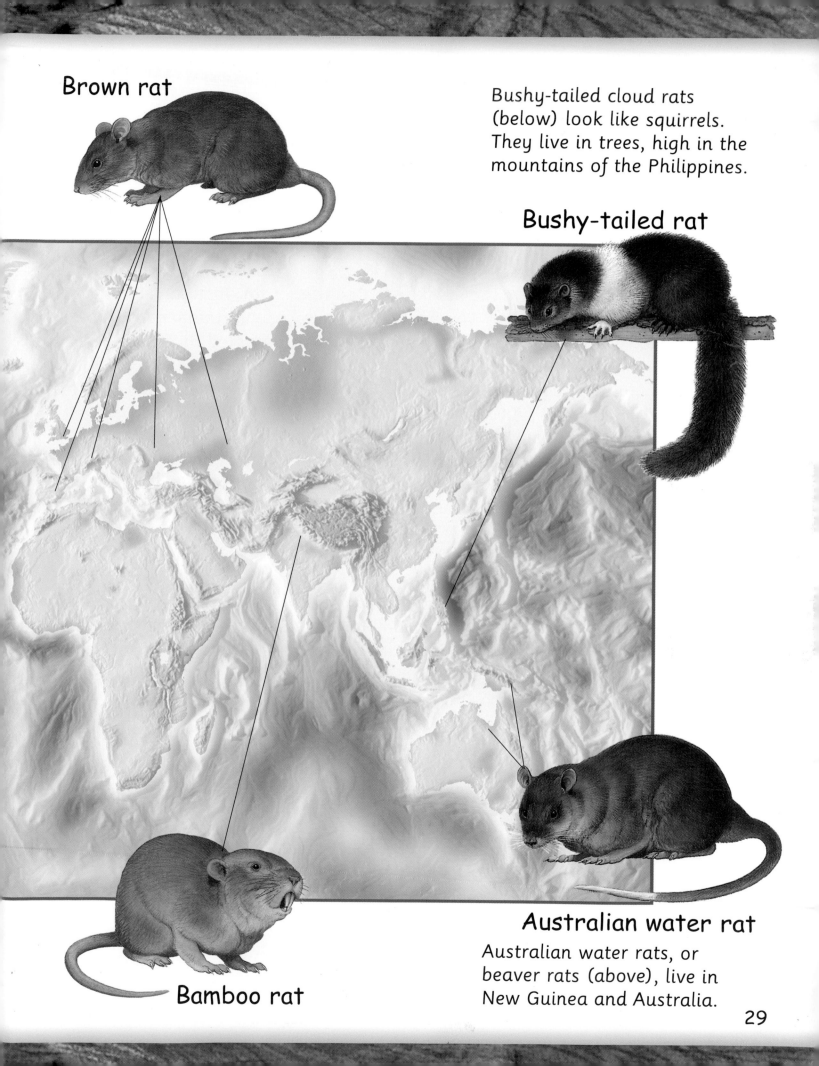

Brown rat

Bushy-tailed cloud rats (below) look like squirrels. They live in trees, high in the mountains of the Philippines.

Bushy-tailed rat

Australian water rat

Australian water rats, or beaver rats (above), live in New Guinea and Australia.

Bamboo rat

Rat Facts

Female rats are pregnant for 22 days before the birth of their babies. Right after the birth, the mother rat eats the placenta and umbilical cord. The babies wriggle and squeak to stop her from eating them, too.

The Flores giant rat can grow up to 18 inches (45 cm) long. Its tail can measure another 15 inches (37 cm).

In Southeast Asia, barn owls are used to catch wood rats. The rats live on oil palm plantations where they cause a lot of damage to the crops.

Rats have been known to attack human babies and kill them. Several babies are killed each year.

The monkey-footed rats of Southeast Asia have evolved feet that can grasp branches as they climb trees.

Rats can survive for two days swimming in open water and may travel up to 1 mile (2 km).

Chinchilla rats live in the cold of the Andes mountains. They are also called chinchillones, and have thick fur to keep them warm.

Sumatran bamboo rats can weigh as much as 9 pounds (4 kg).

In Victorian England, rat catchers supplied rats for dogs to kill for entertainment. A terrier named Billy set a record when he killed 5,000 rats in less than six minutes.

Just one pair of brown rats are able to produce 15,000 descendants in a year!

In South America, fish-eating rats can catch fish the same size as themselves.

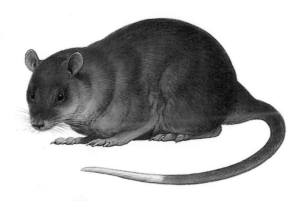

Glossary

adapt Something that has changed to fit a particular purpose.

albino A creature whose coloring is pure white and who has red eyes.

colony A group of animals that live together.

contaminate To pass on dirt or disease.

endangered Animals that are few in numbers and may be close to extinction.

environment The surroundings where an animal lives.

epidemic The fast spread of a disease in an area.

extinct Species of animals that are no longer alive anywhere in the world.

grooming Cleaning hair, fur, or feathers.

habitat The particular environment where an animal lives.

mammal An animal that feeds on its mother's milk when it is a baby.

nocturnal An animal that is active at night.

parasite Tiny living things which live in or on another creature.

pied Black and white.

plague A disease that spreads quickly and kills many people.

predator An animal that hunts other living creatures for food.

prey Any animal that is hunted by other animals for food.

species A group of living things that look alike, behave in the same way, and can interbreed.

wean To gradually stop feeding a young creature milk as it eats more and more solid food.

Index